P9-DFP-652

PUZZLEMANIA®
→Travel Puzzles

HIGHLIGHTS PRESS

Honesdale, Pennsylvania

CONTENTS

When you finish a puzzle, check it off √.
Good luck, and happy puzzling!

Do the Math

Hidden Pictures®

Wordplay

Look Twice

A-Mazing!

Travel Q's

State Your Name

Use the state nicknames to fill in this crossword two letters at a time. Each answer is a state abbreviation. We've filled in the first one. Can you deliver the rest?

1 N	2 C		
	3	4	
		5	6
		7	8

Down

2 Golden State
4 Ocean State
6 Last Frontier
8 Palmetto State
10 Buckeye State
12 Hoosier State
14 Old Dominion State

Across

1 Tar Heel State
3 Natural State
5 Hawkeye State
7 Sunflower State
9 Centennial State
11 Aloha State
13 Silver State
15 Grand Canyon State

In Charge

Molly's electric car is about to run out of battery power! Can you help her get to the charger in time? Just one route will take you there. See if you can find it. And hurry!

Start

SLOW
CURVE
TURN

RECYCLE

Finish

RECYCLE

Illustrated by Garry Colby

7

Surf's UP!

Riley and Sebastian are catching some excellent waves today. While they boogie in to shore, see if you can find at least **20** differences between these two pictures.

Can you find somebody
wearing these swim trunks?

Capital Letters

Pack your bags. We're heading to Europe! The names of **36** capital cities in Europe are hidden in this grid. Tour up, down, across, backwards, and diagonally to see how many you can find. Only the words in capital letters are hidden. Bon voyage!

Word List

AMSTERDAM, Netherlands
ATHENS, Greece
BAKU, Azerbaijan
BELGRADE, Serbia
BERLIN, Germany
BERN, Switzerland
BRUSSELS, Belgium
BUCHAREST, Romania
BUDAPEST, Hungary
COPENHAGEN, Denmark
DUBLIN, Ireland
HELSINKI, Finland
KIEV, Ukraine
LONDON, United Kingdom
LUXEMBOURG, Luxembourg
MADRID, Spain
MINSK, Belarus
MOSCOW, Russia
OSLO, Norway

PARIS, France
PRAGUE, Czech Republic
REYKJAVIK, Iceland
RIGA, Latvia
ROME, Italy
SARAJEVO, Bosnia and Herzegovina
SOFIA, Bulgaria
STOCKHOLM, Sweden
TALLINN, Estonia
TBILISI, Georgia
TIRANA, Albania
VADUZ, Liechtenstein
VALLETTA, Malta
VIENNA, Austria
VILNIUS, Lithuania
WARSAW, Poland
ZAGREB, Croatia

```
B U C H A R E S T M A D R I D G
S A R A J E V O K V A T H E N S U
U Q M N O D N O L B E R L I N V
I P U O H E L S I N K I L T Y R
N Y R A S W A R S A W K K E T E
L N S A B C O C A N A R I T I Y
I G T L G M O S L O V B J A X K
V T O E E U L W B M A R B L G J
J B C N E C E Y A L D U E L R A
D I K U E V O D T B U S L I U V
U L H M Y I R P S Y Z S G N O I
B I O I K E Z B E R N E R N B K
L S L N T N Q B P N P L A T M A
I I M S H N U E A G H S D U E I
N N M K R A Y R D L B A E E X F
T A H R I G A G U Y A I G J U O
V A L L E T T A B E K Z W E L S
V R P A R I S Z S L U H M Z N U
```

Travel Trouble

The two big suitcases look the same. How will Cary know which one is his? His passport is stamped in the order he visited six countries. Use that information to figure it out.

CARY McLUGGAGE

PASSPORT

FRANCE
HOLLAND
GERMANY
ITALY
SPAIN
PORTUGAL

HOLLAND
BELGIUM
DER NEDE
NCE

FRANCE
HOLLAND
GERMANY
ITALY
SPAIN
PORTUGAL

FRANCE
HOLLAND
ITALY
GERMANY
SPAIN
PORTUGAL

Tic Tac Row

Each of these lunch carriers has something in common with the other two lunch carriers in the same row. For example, in the first row across all three have handles on top. Look at the other rows across, down, and diagonally. Can you tell what's alike in each row?

Illustrated by Jim Paillot

Lizard Lounging

This desert is a great place to spot lizards. But you have to know where to look! There are **26** lizards all over the scene. Can you find them all?

Illustrated by Kevin Rechin

California Q's

Cali Quiz

Which of these California statements are true and which are false?

1. California's giant sequoias are the largest trees on Earth.

T or F

2. Oregon, Arizona, and Utah all border California.

T or F

3. More people live in California than in any other U.S. state.

T or F

4. California is home to hundreds of scenic beaches. Three of them are Redondo, Venice, and Daytona.

T or F

FreeWay Free-For-ALL

Can you help Carl drive the freeways around Los Angeles to get home in time for dinner?

Finish

Start

Illustrated by Mike Moran

Film Feature

California is famous for its movies and movie stars. Write down your five favorite movies here.

1. _____
2. _____
3. _____
4. _____
5. _____

16

Missing Vowels

Lndmrks is the word **landmarks** with the vowels taken away. Can you figure out the names of these famous California lndmrks?

HLLYWD
_____

YSMT NTNL PRK
_____

DTH VLLY
_____

LCTRZ
_____

BG SR
_____

Bridge Twins

San Francisco's Golden Gate Bridge is one of the most famous landmarks in the United States. Which two pictures of the bridge match exactly?

A

B

C

D

A Wild Ride

California has lots of fun amusement parks. One park needs your help to design a brand-new ride. Draw it here.

Puzzles by Carly Schuna

Hidden Pictures®
Beach Read

handbell

ring

apple core

pennant

toothbrush

tack

artist's brush

hatchet

pencil

paper clip

tube of toothpaste

flashlight

wedge of orange

needle

snake

banana

magnifying glass

18

Family Vacations

Three families went on vacation. The Kings, the Greens, and the Peñas each have two children, and each family went to a different place. Use the clues to figure out where each family went and what the children's last names are.

Use the chart to keep track of your answers.

For example, the first clue says that William's last name is Green.

Write "Green" in the last name box for William.

	Jennifer	Daniel	Mia	William	Mike	Emily
Last Name						
New York City						
Hawaii						
Alaska						

1. William's last name is Green.
2. The Peña children's names begin with M.
3. Emily and Daniel went to the same place.
4. The King children brought back shells for souvenirs.
5. Jennifer bought a model of the Statue of Liberty.

There's a fish in here somewhere ...

19

CrISSCroSS the U.S.A.

We've scoured the country and found **25** landmarks to place in this puzzle. They can fit in the grid just one way. Use the number of letters in each name to figure out where it belongs. Write in each landmark and cross it off the list as you go. Happy travels!

6 Letters
BIG SUR
COLOMA
DENALI

8 Letters
THE ALAMO
ALCATRAZ
BIG BASIN
FORT KNOX
HALF DOME
SALT LAKE
WIND CAVE

9 Letters
HOOVER DAM
MESA VERDE
PIKES PEAK

10 Letters
DELTA QUEEN
WHITE HOUSE

11 Letters
DEATH VALLEY
GRAND CANYON
MOUNT VERNON
SPACE NEEDLE

12 Letters
FALLINGWATER
HEARST CASTLE
NIAGARA FALLS
PLYMOUTH ROCK

14 Letters
~~BROOKLYN BRIDGE~~

15 Letters
STATUE OF LIBERTY

BROOKLYNBRIDGE

BONUS PUZZLE

Have you filled in all the words? Now write the shaded letters, in order from left to right and top to bottom, in the spaces below to answer this question.

What U.S. attraction is all it's cracked up to be?

___ ___ ___ ___   ___ ___ ___ ___ ___ ___ ___   ___ ___ ___ ___ ___

21

An "IN-teNtS" Trip

All the campers are pitching in to pitch their tents. Can you find at least 25 odd, weird, or wacky things in this picture?

Illustrated by Steve Skelton

Time Piece

Figure out how many minutes are in each of the equations in the box on the left. (Remember, each hour has 60 minutes.) Then shade in each answer you get on the tower. Once you're finished, you should see a clock face in the shaded squares. What time is it, according to the clock?

$\frac{1}{2}$ hour + 3 minutes

$\frac{1}{4}$ hour + 10 minutes

$\frac{3}{4}$ hour

1 hour – 2 minutes

25 minutes + 12 minutes

$\frac{1}{2}$ hour – 4 minutes

10 minutes + 40 minutes + 5 minutes

1 hour + 8 minutes

100 minutes – 16 minutes

$\frac{3}{4}$ hour + 3 minutes

50 minutes + 35 minutes

$\frac{1}{2}$ hour – 6 minutes

1 hour + 2 minutes

45 minutes + 15 minutes + 13 minutes

$\frac{3}{4}$ hour – 3 minutes

1 hour – 8 minutes

62 minutes + $\frac{1}{4}$ hour

80 minutes – 24 minutes

1 hour – 25 minutes

$1\frac{1}{2}$ hours – 4 minutes

Illustrated by Ron Zalme

Hidden Pictures®
Hello, Lady Liberty

kite

dog's head

book

fork

closed umbrella

harp

comb

spoon

doorknob

ladle

toothbrush

glove

26

Can you find the hidden objects? When you finish, you can color in the rest of the scene.

pitcher

horn

high-heeled shoe

pear

cookie jar

slipper

teapot

sock

teacup

golf club

canoe

eyeglasses

pillow

banana

snail

Illustrated by Kathy Swain-O'Brien

27

The Waiting Game

Everyone is waiting to board a plane. Before they take off, see if you can find at least **20** differences between these pictures.

Find the two airplanes that match exactly.

Illustrated by Dave Clegg

Lost Luggage

Sandy has lost her luggage at the airport! Help her find it in the lost luggage room.

START

FINISH

Illustrated by Mike Dammer

31

Park Here

The United States has dozens of national parks. The names of **33** are hidden in these letters. Can you find them all? They are hidden up, down, across, backwards, and diagonally. (The state abbreviations are not hidden.)

Word List

ACADIA (ME)
ARCHES (UT)
BADLANDS (SD)
BIG BEND (TX)
BISCAYNE (FL)
CONGAREE (SC)
CRATER LAKE (OR)
DENALI (AK)
DRY TORTUGAS (FL)
EVERGLADES (FL)
GLACIER BAY (AK)
GRAND CANYON (AZ)
GRAND TETON (WY)
GREAT BASIN (NV)
GREAT SMOKY
  MOUNTAINS (NC, TN)
HALEAKALA (HI)
HOT SPRINGS (AR)
ISLE ROYALE (MI)
JOSHUA TREE (CA)
KATMAI (AK)
MAMMOTH CAVE (KY)
MESA VERDE (CO)
MOUNT RAINIER (WA)
OLYMPIC (WA)
REDWOOD (CA)
ROCKY MOUNTAIN (CO)
SAGUARO (AZ)
SEQUOIA (CA)
SHENANDOAH (VA)
WIND CAVE (SD)
YELLOWSTONE (ID, MT, WY)
YOSEMITE (CA)
ZION (UT)

S Z N G R A N D C A N Y O N E S M
N I P M O U N T R A I N I E R N A
O O R O R T E L A Y O R E L S I M
Y N D R Y T O R T U G A S Y N A M
R O S A L A K A E L A H G E G T O
O W S E D A L G R E V E A L R N T
C C I E D E N A L I E G J L E U H
K K O N M A T R A P N R O O A O C
Y E R N D I S D K B Y I C W T M A
M R S T G C T E E I A X I S B Y V
O J K L Z A A E F G C Y P T A K E
U I O V O I R V S B S R M O S O B
N A J S D U R E E E I S Y N I M A
T M E A H E Q J E N B G L E N S D
A T C G D U C D G D B J O Q Z T L
I A N W O R A S A G U A R O B A A
N K O I A N O T E T D N A R G E N
X O A B V Y A B R E I C A L G R D
D Y H A O D N A N E H S S I V G S
M E S A V E R D E S E H C R A O B

Australia Q's

Return to Sender

Chet is waiting for his boomerang to return. Can you find a path from START to FINISH so that Chet can make his catch?

Finish

Start

Illustrated by Mike Moran

Dive IN!

The Great Barrier Reef is the world's largest coral reef. Lots of fish can be found in it—and so can lots of words! How many words can you make from the letters in **GREAT BARRIER REEF?**

_____   _____   _____

_____   _____   _____

_____   _____   _____

ANiMaL MiX-UP!

A platypus has a bill like a duck, a tail like a beaver, and fur like an otter. Draw your own mixed-up animal here.

'Doo This

A **didgeridoo** is a native Australian instrument. Can you find the doo that doesn't match the other two?

ANiMaLS oR NoT?

Each pair of words has one Australian animal and one imposter. Circle the animals.

Mumu OR **Emu?**

Ringo OR **Dingo?**

Koala OR **Kudzu?**

Wombat OR **Dingbat?**

Wannabee OR **Wallaby?**

Kookaburra OR **Chimichanga?**

Aussie Speak

G'day, mate! How many of these Australian words can you fit into one sentence?

arvo	afternoon
barby	a barbecue
billabong	water hole
bonzer	excellent, great
outback	remote part of Australia

_____

_____

_____

Sun and Shades

It's a perfect day for the beach—and for trying out those new sunglasses! Shade your eyes and look carefully. There are **five pairs** of sunglasses that match exactly. Can you find them all?

36

Illustrated by Geneviève Kote

37

Digit Does It

For his vacation this year, Inspector Digit took his niece and nephew to the shore. They knew the inspector was going to look for shells to add to his collection. On the first morning of his search, the inspector was shocked to see that all the shells

were missing from the beach. All he could find was this coded message in a bottle. Can you decode the message and help Digit find the missing shells? The first line reads **"Dear Uncle."**

$\overline{14}\ \overline{18}\ \overline{1}\ \overline{16}\quad \overline{9}\ \overline{8}\ \overline{10}\ \overline{3}\ \overline{18},$

$\overline{14}\ \overline{12}\ \overline{8}\ \overline{4},\quad \overline{6}\ \overline{18}\quad \overline{20}\ \overline{11}\ \overline{12}\ \overline{10}\ \overline{19}\ \overline{18}\ \overline{14},$

$\overline{6}\ \overline{9}\ \overline{4}\quad \overline{17}\ \overline{18}\quad \overline{11}\ \overline{15}\ \overline{14}\quad \overline{1}\ \overline{3}\ \overline{3}\quad \overline{4}\ \overline{11}\ \overline{18}$

$\overline{20}\ \overline{11}\ \overline{18}\ \overline{3}\ \overline{3}\ \overline{20}.\quad \overline{5}\ \overline{12}\ \overline{9}\ \overline{3}\ \overline{3},\quad \overline{11}\ \overline{1}\ \overline{13}\ \overline{18}$

$\overline{4}\ \overline{12}\quad \overline{18}\ \overline{21}\ \overline{18}\ \overline{16}\ \overline{10}\ \overline{15}\ \overline{20}\ \overline{18}\quad \overline{5}\ \overline{12}\ \overline{9}\ \overline{16}$

"$\overline{20}\ \overline{11}\ \overline{18}\ \overline{3}\ \overline{3}\ \overline{2}\quad \overline{10}\ \overline{12}\ \overline{8}\ \overline{4}\ \overline{16}\ \overline{12}\ \overline{3}$"-$\quad \overline{4}\ \overline{12}$

$\overline{2}\ \overline{15}\ \overline{8}\ \overline{14}\quad \overline{1}\ \overline{3}\ \overline{3}\quad \overline{F}\ \overline{Y}.$

"$\overline{20}\ \overline{12}\ \overline{16}\ \overline{16}\ \overline{5}\quad \overline{4}\ \overline{12}\quad \overline{6}\ \overline{18}\quad \overline{20}\ \overline{12}$

$\overline{20}\ \overline{11}\ \overline{18}\ \overline{3}\ \overline{3}$"-$\quad \overline{2}\ \overline{15}\ \overline{20}\ \overline{11}.$

$\overline{3}\ \overline{12}\ \overline{13}\ \overline{18},$

$\overline{14}\ \overline{18}\ \overline{8}\ \overline{15}\ \overline{20}\ \overline{18}\quad \overline{1}\ \overline{8}\ \overline{14}$

$\overline{14}\ \overline{18}\ \overline{8}\ \overline{18}\ \overline{2}\ \overline{2}\ \overline{18}\ \overline{17}\quad \overline{14}\ \overline{15}\ \overline{7}\ \overline{15}\ \overline{4}$

Illustrated by John Nez

Seeing i to i

Twenty-eight states have the letter **i** in their names. Use your keen puzzle-solving eyes to fill in the grid with each of these state names. Remember to keep your eyes peeled for the length of each name. That will help you figure out where to put each state. The **i**'s are already in place to get you started.

4 Letters
IOWA
OHIO

5 Letters
IDAHO
MAINE

6 Letters
HAWAII

7 Letters
ARIZONA
FLORIDA
GEORGIA
INDIANA
WYOMING

8 Letters
ILLINOIS
MICHIGAN
MISSOURI
VIRGINIA

9 Letters
LOUISIANA
MINNESOTA
NEW MEXICO
WISCONSIN

10 Letters
CALIFORNIA
WASHINGTON

11 Letters
CONNECTICUT
MISSISSIPPI
RHODE ISLAND

12 Letters
NEW HAMPSHIRE
PENNSYLVANIA
WEST VIRGINIA

13 Letters
NORTH CAROLINA
SOUTH CAROLINA

Idaho

Maine

Florida

Pennsylvania

Wisconsin

Illustrated by Terry Taylor

41

COUNTRY Sudoku

Grab your passport—we're heading around the world! Each grid holds one country. Fill in the boxes so that each row, column, and six-letter section contains the letters of that country. We've filled in some of the letters to get you started. Can you fill in the rest?

France grid:

F	R	A	N	C	E
		C	A		R
R			C	N	
N	C			E	A
		R		A	N
		N	F		

Turkey grid:

T	U	R	K	E	Y
E				K	E
	E		T		R
	R	T	E		
Y					
R			Y	U	K

Brazil grid:

B	R	A	Z	I	L
Z					B
	B	I			
I	L	R		Z	A
A	B	I		L	I
	I		A	B	Z

Hidden Pictures
A Tall Taxi

Illustrated by Ron Lieser

envelope

boot

saw

mallet

wedge of apple

glove

bell

canoe

hot dog

snake

comb

frying pan

pliers

tweezers

oilcan

heart

43

To New Depths

Captain Nemo has been taking his new submarine out for experimental dives. Can you help him complete his log for each day? Can you find the total of his dives for the week? Use a ruler to

LOG

Monday
Only got as deep as a crab on a rock. Managed to reach a depth of approximately ___ feet.

Tuesday
Managed to reach the level of the top of the hull of a wreck. Reached close to ___ feet.

Wednesday
An octopus barred my way. Went to a depth of ___ feet.

Thursday
The approach of a giant jellyfish stopped my dive at ___ feet.

Friday
Reached the bottom. Ship stopped at ___ feet.

0 feet

1" = 50 feet

50 feet

Total for the week: ___ feet

44

measure the distance straight down from the surface to each X. Then translate your measurements in inches to feet. (You'll see that 1 inch = 50 feet, according to the key in the yellow box.)

Beware Bears

It's salmon spawning time in Alaska, and the bears are everywhere!
Help this family get back to their lodge safely.

START

FINISH

Illustrated by Larry Jones

Hidden Pictures®
Pier Cheer

Illustrated by Dave Klug

There is more than meets the eye on this town pier. Can you find the hidden objects?

envelope

boomerang

pumpkin

ear of corn

rake

book

golf club

ruler

baseball bat

horseshoe

candle

slice of pizza

pencil

pliers

saucepan

saltshaker

comb

waffle

pitcher

mitten

sock

ring

scarf

banana

hanger

hockey stick

Rapid Repeat

Look out! This raft is heading straight for Rollercoaster Rapids. Before everyone gets soaked, see if you can find at least **20** differences between these pictures.

Which fish matches the one on this page?

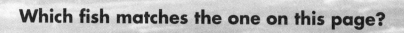

Illustrated by Brian White

51

City Q's

Guess What?

Can you figure out what famous landmark is in this picture and what West Coast city it's from?

Europe or Asia?

Some of these cities are from Europe and some are from Asia. Can you figure out which are which?

LONDON	**MUMBAI**
TOKYO	**MADRID**
PARIS	**BANGKOK**
AMSTERDAM	**VENICE**
HONG KONG	**SEOUL**

Also Known As...

Can you match each U.S. city with its nickname?

CHICAGO ●	● **THE BIG APPLE**
DETROIT ●	● **THE BIG EASY**
NASHVILLE ●	● **THE WINDY CITY**
NEW ORLEANS ●	● **THE CITY OF BROTHERLY LOVE**
NEW YORK CITY ●	● **MOTOWN**
PHILADELPHIA ●	● **MUSIC CITY**

52

RUSH HOUR

Can you help Austin reach his subway train before it leaves?

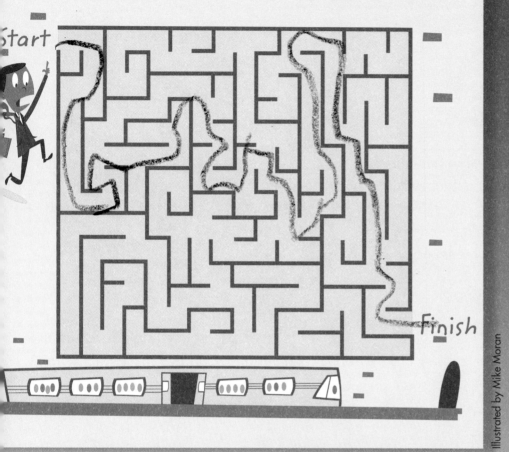

Start

Finish

Illustrated by Mike Moran

Twin Taxis

Which two taxi cabs are exactly alike?

A

B

C

D

Maryland

JUMBLED CITIES

Unscramble each set of letters to get the name of a city.

LET'S EAT, Washington ⎯ ⎯ ⎯ ⎯ ⎯ ⎯ ⎯

ALL SAD, Texas ⎯ ⎯ ⎯ ⎯ ⎯ ⎯

BROIL MEAT, Maryland ⎯ ⎯ ⎯ ⎯ ⎯ ⎯ ⎯ ⎯ ⎯

NACHO GEAR, Alaska ⎯ ⎯ ⎯ ⎯ ⎯ ⎯ ⎯ ⎯ ⎯

NO EMAIL PINS, Minnesota ⎯ ⎯ ⎯ ⎯ ⎯ ⎯ ⎯ ⎯ ⎯ ⎯ ⎯

Tugboat Travels

This tugboat tours the channels around Howe's Bayou. But the captain has another job to do when he gets back: getting the elephants off Ivory Key and

Dock 1: The captain is pulling out with three passengers. Put an X in the blank that matches the number of people on board. *(Don't forget to count the captain!)*

Island 2:
One man gets off. One man and one woman get on. Put a T in the blank that matches the number of people now on board.

Island 3: Three people get off to pick strawberries. Put an N in the blank that matches the number of people on board now.

Island 5: The captain delivers mail to this island, and two more people get on. Put a B in the blank that matches the number of people on board now.

Island 4: Three people get on with fishing poles. One man gets off, but then two women get on. Just as the tug is about to leave, one more man jumps on. Put an L in the blank that matches the number of people on board now.

POST OFFICE

bringing them to their new home on Jumbo Laya Key. Follow the instructions at each stop and you will discover the kind of boat that he should use.

Island 6: One woman gets off to visit a sick friend. Put a G in the blanks that match the number of people on board now.

Island 9: The last passengers get off as the tugboat heads home. Put an A in the blanks that match the number of people on board now.

Island 7: Two people get off to go hiking. Put an R in the blanks that match the number of people on board now.

Island 8: Two people decide this would be a good place for a picnic, so they get off. One woman also disembarks to pick wild flowers. Put an E in the blanks that match the number of people on board now.

Illustrated by Scott Peck

What kind of boat will the captain use to move the elephants?

$$\frac{}{1} \ \frac{}{2} \ \frac{}{3} \ \frac{}{4} \ \frac{}{5} \ \frac{}{6} \ \frac{}{1} \ \ - \ \ \frac{}{7} \ \frac{}{1} \ \frac{}{6} \ \frac{}{8} \ \frac{}{3}$$

$$\frac{}{9} \ \frac{}{1} \ \frac{}{6} \ \frac{}{8} \ \frac{}{3}$$

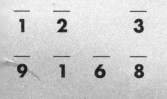

Castle Search

There are **35** European castles hidden in this grid. Look up, down, across, backwards, and diagonally to find the names. Only the words in capital letters are hidden. Have a royally good time!

Illustrated by Wendy Wax

Word List

ARDENNE (Belgium)
BEESTON (England)
BERAT (Albania)
BORY (Hungary)
BRAN (Romania)
BRODICK (Scotland)
CHAMBORD (France)
CHILLON (Switzerland)
DOORNENBURG (Denmark)
DOVER (England)
DUBOVAC (Croatia)
ELTZ (Germany)
FRANKENSTEIN (Germany)
GISORS (France)
LINCOLN (England)
LOARRE (Spain)
MAMER (Luxembourg)
MOLD (Wales)

MOYRY (Ireland)
PIEL (England)
RHOON (Netherlands)
ROSENBURG (Austria)
ROSKILDE (Denmark)
RUFUS (England)
SARZANA (Italy)
SWINY (Poland)
THUN (Switzerland)
TOOLSE (Estonia)
USK (Wales)
VITRE (France)
WELL (Netherlands)
WIK (Sweden)
WINDSOR (England)
ZATOR (Poland)
ZENA (Italy)

56

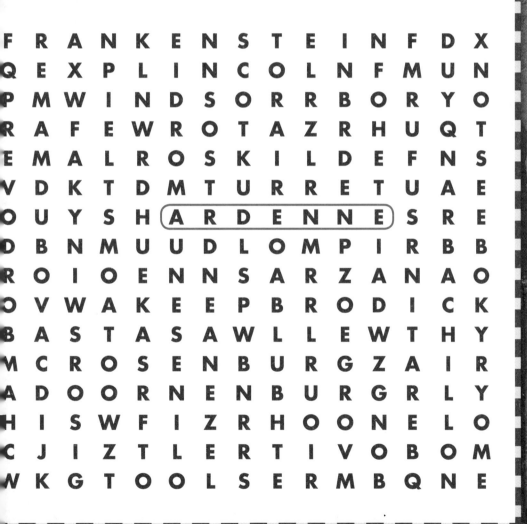

```
F R A N K E N S T E I N F D X
Q E X P L I N C O L N F M U N
P M W I N D S O R R B O R Y O
R A F E W R O T A Z R H U Q T
E M A L R O S K I L D E F N S
V D K T D M T U R R E T U A E
O U Y S H (A R D E N N E) S R E
D B N M U U D L O M P I R B B
R O I O E N N S A R Z A N A O
O V W A K E E P B R O D I C K
B A S T A S A W L L E W T H Y
M C R O S E N B U R G Z A I R
A D O O R N E N B U R G R L Y
H I S W F I Z R H O O N E L O
C J I Z T L E R T I V O B O M
N K G T O O L S E R M B Q N E
```

57

Awesome, Dude!

Everyone is ridin' and ropin' at the Lazy Grazer Dude Ranch. Can you find at least **25** odd, weird, or wacky things in this picture?

Illustrated by Tim Haggerty

L.G.
Dud Ranch

LEAVE YOUR BIG CITY IDEAS HERE.

Hidden Pictures®
A Whale of a Time

There is more than meets the eye on this whale-watching boat. Can you find the hidden objects?

sock

star

whistle

mitten

butterfly

ring

mushroom

bottle

crescent moon

ladle

tennis racket

carrot

boomerang

mallet

radish

ghost

apple

comb

mouse

teacup

magnifying glass

adhesive bandage

candle

banana

scarf

toothbrush

baseball

ruler

hot-air balloon

cloud

61

Mayan Maze

The Murray family are vacationing in Mexico and visiting the famous pyramids. Help them climb to the top by finding a path.

Start

Finish

Illustrated by Dave Garbot

On Sail

It's the annual boat parade, and all sorts of sailboats have joined in the fun. Floating in this sea of sails are three pairs of matching boats. Can you find them? Hurry, before they sail away!

USA 55

USA 92361 SKI

USA 93621 SKY

21

33 US

USA 64

USA 55

USA

USA 55 USA 55

21

33 US

Illustrated by Wendy Wax

65

saucepan

slice of pie

banana

nail

sock

mitten

hammer

fish

sheep

needle

pair of pants

butter knife

drinking straw

cane

Tic Tac Row

Each of these lighthouses has something in common with the other two lighthouses in the same row. For example, in the top row across each lighthouse has a black roof. Look at the other rows across, down, and diagonally. Can you tell what's alike in each row?

Illustrated by Garry Colby

Hidden Pictures®
Wild Times

Illustrated by Kevin Rechin

**There is more than meets the eye on this safari.
Can you find the hidden objects?**

baseball glove

kite

envelope

mouse

fish

baseball bat

book

flying saucer

pencil

fishhook

button

spoon

lock

sailboat

party hat

fried egg

paper clip

banana

bell

boomerang

canoe

Hawaii Q's

Hawaii or Not?

Each pair of words has one Hawaiian city or island and one faker. Circle the real parts of Hawaii.

Hilo OR **Hello?**

Zowie OR **Maui?**

Kauai OR **Walleye?**

Oahu OR **Ah-choo?**

Waipahu OR **Weimaraner?**

Mogadishu OR **Honolulu?**

Cola OR **Kona?**

Hot Hike

Hawaii is a good place to climb a volcano. Can you help the hiker get to the top of this one?

Finish

Start

Illustrated by Mike Moran

TWiN LEiS

Leis made of flowers are given to visitors as a traditional Hawaiian welcome. Which two of these are exactly alike?

B

D

A

C

Map It Out

Hawaii is the only U.S. state made up of islands. If you could create your own island, what would it look like? Draw your map here.

Missing Vowels

TRPCL FRTS are the words *tropical fruits* with the vowels taken away. Can you figure out the names of these five trpcl frts that grow in Hawaii?

_____
BNN

_____
PNPPL

_____
CCNT

_____
MNG

_____
PSSN FRT

Aloha!

How many of these Hawaiian words can you fit into one sentence?

Honu — turtle
Nui — big
Kai — sea
Wai — water
Wikiwiki — fast

_____

_____

_____

Lodging Logic

It's vacation time and a lot of families are on the road. Use the clues to determine the hotel in which each family is spending the night. Here's a tip: Begin by figuring out where the Princes are staying.

The Rhodes
Their hotel is between the Dukes' and the Travellis'.

The Karrs
They are sleeping in the hotel next to the Quinns'.

The O'Nighters
Their hotel address is all odd numbers.

The Kings
The address of their hotel can be counted exactly halfway between the highest address and the lowest address.

The Quinns
Their hotel address is three consecutive numbers in order.

The Dukes
Their hotel address is less than the address of the O'Nighters' hotel.

The Princes
They are staying in the last hotel on the right side of the highway.

The Travellis
They are staying in an even-numbered hotel.

World Pieces

We've whipped up a batch of scrambled countries just for you. The letters in each of these phrases can be rearranged to spell the name of a country. How many can you unscramble?

1. A CAN AD (North America) C A N A D A

2. A CHIN (Asia) _ _ _ _ _

3. WE SEND (Europe) _ _ _ _ _ _

4. KEY RUT (Middle East) _ _ _ _ _ _

5. REAL DIN (Europe) _ _ _ _ _ _ _

6. ANGRY ME (Europe) _ _ _ _ _ _ _

7. A HAND LIT (Asia) _ _ _ _ _ _ _ _

8. HI OAT PIE (Africa) _ _ _ _ _ _ _ _

9. CACTI OARS (Central America) _ _ _ _ _ _
_ _ _ _

10. I SEAT STUDENT (North America) _ _ _ _ _ _
_ _ _ _ _

11. HAIRCUT OAFS (Africa) _ _ _ _ _ _
_ _ _ _ _ _

12. NEAR GIANT (South America)
_ _ _ _ _ _ _ _ _

Aloha!

Howdy! Fourteen ways to say hello from around the world are listed here. Each greeting will fit into the grid in just one way. Use the number of letters in a greeting to help figure out where it will fit. Only the words in capital letters go in the grid.

Word List

BONJOUR (French)
~~CIAO~~ **(Italian)**
~~G'DAY~~ **(Australian)**
GOD DAG (Swedish)
GUTEN TAG (German)
~~HOLA~~ **(Spanish)**
JAMBO (Swahili)
KONNICHI WA (Japanese)
NAMASTE (Hindi)
NI HAO (Cantonese)
SALAAM (Arabic)
SHALOM (Hebrew)
WITAJ (Polish)
YIA SAS (Greek)

Rolling on the River

Help Kayak Jack and his faithful dog, Buster, paddle all the way down Rio Splasho. The letters on the correct path will spell the answer to the riddle waiting at the FINISH dock.

C

O

N

G

F

T

P

E

X

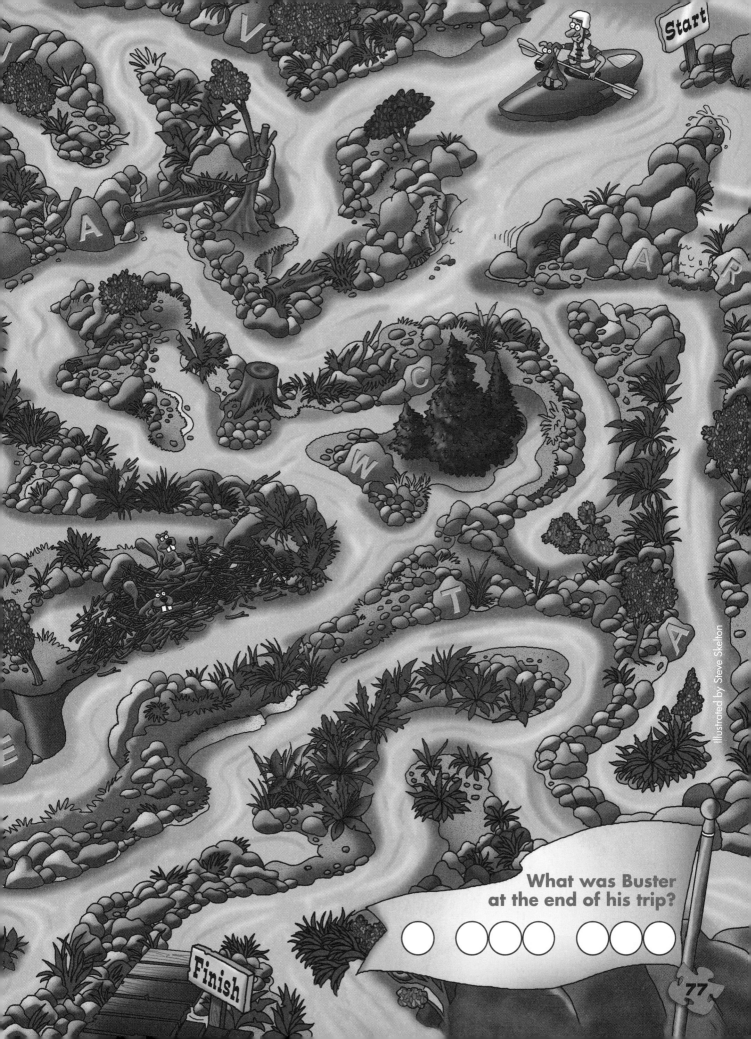

Start

What was Buster
at the end of his trip?

○ ○○○ ○○○

Finish

77

Hidden Pictures
Zoo View

78

There is more than meets the eye at this zoo. Can you find the hidden objects?

jump rope

sock

fish

bird

carrot

paintbrush

loaf of bread

paper clip

teacup

dog

banana

seashell

caterpillar

toothbrush

key

shoe

bowling pin

ring

whale

glove

rake

golf club

golf tee

pennant

Ferry Funny

Ahoy! There are some strange sights at the ferry dock today. Can you find at least **25** odd, weird, or wacky things in this picture?

81

Map Miles

Trip 1—Eagle Tower to Sandtown   _____ miles

Trip 2—Wood to Lakeside   _____ miles

Trip 3—Blue City to Cedar Springs   _____ miles

Trip 4—Big Bay to Blufftown   _____ miles

Trip 5—Rapid River to Rockville   _____ miles

Myles Tugo is hitting the road. Can you look at his map and help him add up the shortest routes between the towns he will visit?

Italy Search

Buongiorno! We've collected **35** words that have to do with Italy. There are cities, foods, historic sites, famous Italians, and more. To find them, look up, down, across, backwards, and diagonally. Have fun! *Ciao!*

Word List

ALPS	MARINARA	RAVIOLI
ARNO	MICHELANGELO	RISOTTO
CAESAR	MILAN	ROME
CANNOLI	NAPLES	SARDINIA
CIAO	OPERA	SICILY
COLOSSEUM	PANTHEON	SISTINE CHAPEL
DA VINCI	PESTO	TUSCANY
FLORENCE	PIAZZA	VATICAN
GALILEO	PISA	VENICE
GELATO	PIZZA	VESUVIUS
GRAZIE	POMPEII	VILLA
LASAGNA	RAPHAEL	

G A L I L E O O T T O S I R P
G R E E N C O L O S S E U M A N
N A L I M G E L A T O L V I N
F L O R E N C E L D R P A Q T H
W P E S T O Y E O A L A T H E
H S I M U N A V S V E N I C E N
I P I S A H C E D I P B C A O
T O I C P B A S M N A R A K N
E F S A O C N U A C H L N U I
R U R R M A N V Z I C A J A L
T O B E P R O I Z N E C I A O
K O M D E E L U A V N N N Q L I V
L U R E I P I S I C I L Y D V A
F L A G I O O V P D T L Y Y A
C L A Z Z I P N R Q S Q L C R
M A R I N A R A R T I E A A H
E I Z A R G S X L A S A G N A
M I C H E L A N G E L O B G I

Family Ties

Five cousins met at a family reunion. Each comes from a different state, and each is a different age. From the clues below, can you figure out each cousin's age and home state?

Use the chart to keep track of your answers. Put an **X** in each box that can't be true and an **O** in boxes that match.

	New York	New Mexico	Maine	California	Iowa	6	8	9	10	12
Alyssa										
Brad										
Catie										
Daniel										
Eve										

1. Alyssa is twice as old as her cousin from Maine.

2. The 8-year-old, who has the shortest name, is from the state with the most letters in its name.

3. Daniel is from a state in New England.

4. The 10-year-old's name and state have the same number of letters.

5. Alyssa told her cousins about her favorite place in her home state: the Statue of Liberty.

Hidden Pictures®
Aerial View

ice-cream cone

slice of pizza

sock

domino

teacup

adhesive bandage

snowman

crayon

fish

snowcone

snake

ball of yarn

party hat

pencil

wedge of lemon

Illustrated by Susan T. Hall

87

Pool Plunge

Nat's family just checked into their hotel. Can you help him find the way to the pool?

Start

Finish

Illustrated by Mike Moran

Puzzles by Lori Mortensen

WHere AM I?

These vacation sights got mismatched! Can you figure out which first word goes with which second word and put the places back together again?

Liberty Canyon
Space Bell
Grand Falls
Niagara Rock
Plymouth Needle

_____

_____

_____

_____

_____

JUMBLed PaCKiNG

Unscramble each set of letters to get the name of something you might pack for vacation.

OKBO ___ ___ ___ ___

STORSH ___ ___ ___ ___ ___ ___

ACREAM ___ ___ ___ ___ ___ ___

ISITSWUM ___ ___ ___ ___ ___ ___ ___ ___

SNAUSSGLES ___ ___ ___ ___ ___ ___ ___ ___ ___ ___

Hit the Road

Can you match each tourist destination with its location?

Lincoln Memorial •   • Wyoming

Old Faithful •   • Texas

Statue of Liberty •   • South Dakota

Mount Rushmore •   • Washington, D.C.

Gateway Arch •   • New York

The Alamo •   • Missouri

PICTURE POSTCARD

Draw a picture of a place you'd like to visit on this postcard.

Trip Trios

Which two suitcase pictures are exactly alike?

Go...Go...Gorilla!

START

Can you help Viola reach the gorillas so she can take photos?
Find a clear path from START to FINISH.

FINISH

Illustrated by Steve Skelton

Digit Does It

That renowned detective, Inspector Digit, has stumbled upon a group of unhappy tourists. Reaching for some coins to call for help, the only thing the inspector found was a coded

note that had been slipped into his pocket. Help him decode the note to learn what crime has occurred. Hint: The first line reads, **"Dear Inspector Digit."**

Illustrated by John Nez

Hidden Pictures®
Coral Explorers

There is more than meets the eye in this coral reef. Can you find the hidden objects?

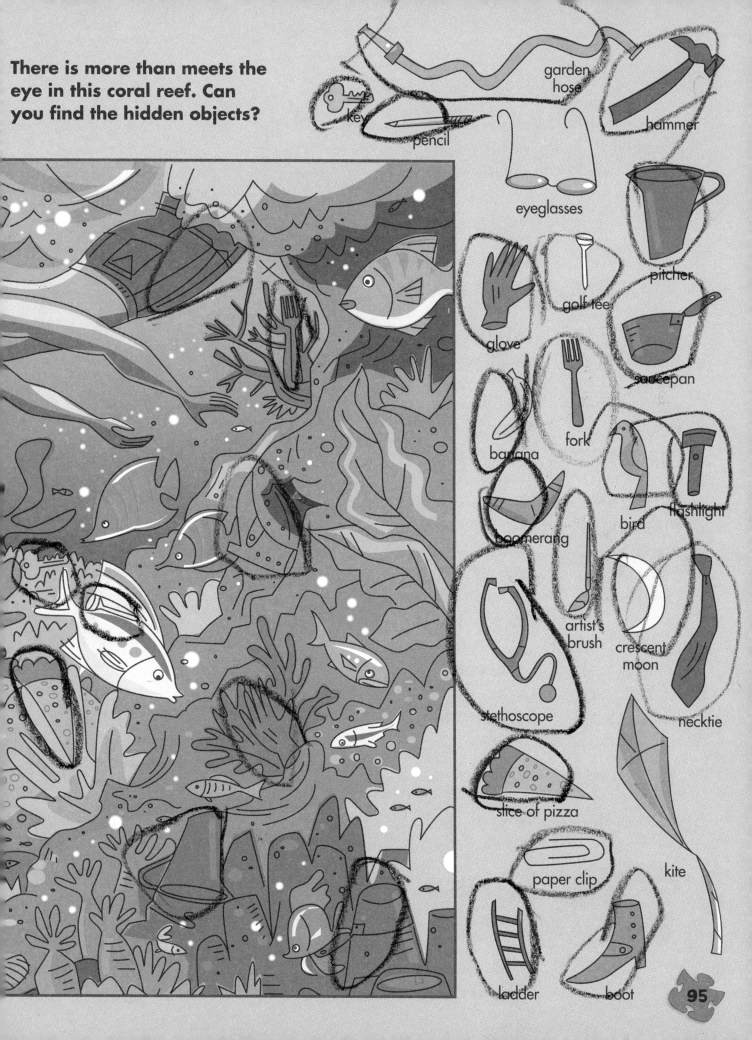

key

pencil

garden hose

hammer

eyeglasses

pitcher

glove

golf tee

saucepan

banana

fork

bird

flashlight

boomerang

artist's brush

crescent moon

stethoscope

necktie

slice of pizza

kite

paper clip

ladder

boot

95

Aussie Animals

G'day, mate! Australia is home to many fascinating animals. You can find 35 hiding "down under" in this grid. Look up, down, across, backwards, and diagonally to find the words. Ready? Hop to it!

Word List

- ~~AMPUTA~~
- BANDICOOT
- BILBY
- BLACK SWAN
- BROLGA
- CASSOWARY
- COCKATOO
- CROCODILE
- DIBBLER
- DINGO
- DUGONG
- ECHIDNA
- EMU
- FAIRY PENGUIN
- FLYING FOX
- GHOST BAT
- KANGAROO
- KINKAJOU
- KOALA
- KOOKABURRA
- KOWARI
- LACE MONITOR
- LORIKEET
- MULGARA
- NUMBAT
- PILLIGA MOUSE
- POTOROO
- QUOKKA
- SKINK
- SUGAR GLIDER
- TASMANIAN DEVIL
- WALLABY
- WALLAROO
- WOMBAT
- YABBY

```
B W B L A C E M O N I T O R D T I
R I E C H I D N A I Q U O K K A N
O B L H K A B R D U C G O O F B U
E L I B L X A I L G D B O O Q M R
S A D A Y D N L R N N R R K E O S
U C O R P G D O O E W O A A E W R
O K C E O C I R M P A D G B O A M
M S O D T O C I A Y L B N U N L U
A W R I O C O K M R L A A R D L L
G A C L R K O E P I A K K R Y A G
I N B G O A T E U A R A T A R B A
L U M R O T W T T F O W G Y A Y R
L M Y A Q O N O A P O U V L W N A
I B A G J O L A K T A B T S O H G
P A B U O J A K N I K N I K S R I
Q T B S K X D I B B L E R F S N B
F L Y I N G F O X K A B O U A F T
T A S M A N I A N D E V I L C G J
```

Island Rides

Aloha Airways Flight 62 has just arrived in this vacation paradise, and the passengers are eager to get to their hotels. The driver from each hotel is holding a sign with an equation.

10 ÷ 2

(2 x 2) x 2 + 2

2 x 2

11 − 2

5 + 2

(2 x 2) x 2

Illustrated by Scott Peck

The answer to each problem is printed on a tourist's shirt, bag, or other item. Can you link the visitors to the correct drivers, so they can all get to their proper destinations?

SHUTTLE

$0 + 2$

$22 \div 2$

$2 \div 2$

$1 + 2$

$(2 \times 2) \times (2 + 1)$

2×3

7

8

9

10

12

Up, Up, and Away!

These pages are heating up! Each hot-air balloon has one that matches it exactly. Can you find each matching pair?

101

Tic Tac Row

Each of these stamps has something in common with the other two stamps in the same row. For example, in the first row down all three stamps have blue backgrounds. Look at the other rows across, down, and diagonally. Can you tell what's alike in each row?

Illustrated by Wendy Wax

Hidden Pictures®
Are We There Yet?

Illustrated by Karen Stormer Brooks

ruler

teacup

ladder

sailboat

golf club

telephone receiver

bird

shoe

bell

fishhook

broom

baseball bat

ring

slice of pizza

Traffic Jamboree

Beep, beep! There are some strange sights at this traffic jam.
Can you find at least **25** odd, weird, or wacky things in this picture?

Illustrated by Tim Haggerty

105

Egypt Q's

On the Nile

Can you help this archeologist find her way down the Nile River to her work site?

Start

Finish

Illustrated by Mike Moran   Puzzles by Carly Schuna

Boy King

King Tut's full name, **TUTANKHAMUN**, is 11 letters long. See if you can make at least 11 words from the letters in it.

_____   _____

_____   _____

_____   _____

_____   _____

_____   _____

_____   _____

Egypt or Not?

Some of these are Egyptian cities and some are cities from other countries. Can you figure out which are which?

Luxor or Lima?

Giza or Pisa?

Tokyo or Cairo?

Istanbul or Ismailia?

Alexandria or Athens?

Suez or Santa Cruz?

Toronto or Tanta?

Write Like an Egyptian

Hieroglyphs are written symbols used by the ancient Egyptians. Here are a few. Try to draw these. Then make up your own!

owl   water   snake

JUMBLed Egypt

Unscramble each set of letters to get a word that has to do with Egypt.

LINE — — — —

YUMMM — — — — —

AHARAS — — — — — —

XSHIPN — — — — — —

DIPRAYM — — — — — — —

Twin Sphinxes

Which two sphinxes are exactly alike?

Island Hopping

The Penningtons have just hopped onto a ferry back to the mainland. Help them navigate through the islands.

O

O

O

T

R

U

Start

A

G

U

Finish

B

F

S

F

F

Bonus Puzzle
Once you've found the correct path, write the letters along it, in order, in the spaces below. They'll answer the riddle.

Why don't dogs like being on boats?

Because the waters are __ __ __ __ __ __ __ !

Illustrated by Nathan Jarvis

Hidden Pictures®
Mount Rushmore

banana

hanger

high-heeled shoe

paper clip

ice-cream cone

spoon

110

goose

2 dolphins

snake

shovel

feather

Can you find the hidden objects?
When you finish, you can color in
the rest of the scene.

open book

sailboat

slice of pie

closed
umbrella

pencil

candle

handbell

heart

Illustrated by Tim Davis

fish

carrot

glove

shoe

T-shirt

On the Road Again

Rhoda travels a lot. Her car gets an average of 30 miles to the gallon. Can you look over her list of stops this week and figure out how far she's going to travel? How much gas will she use? (Rhoda will stay overnight in each town, then drive on to her next destination.)

Illustrated by Scott Peck

Treasure Beach

Jake and five of his friends went to the beach. Each brought something to use, and each found a treasure. From the clues below, can you match each friend with a toy or tool and a treasure?

Use the chart to keep track of your answers. Put an **X** in each box that can't be true and an **O** in boxes that match.

	Jake	Eddie	Braden	Haley	Martha	Kiera
Bucket						
Shovel						
Towel						
Goggles						
Fins						
Cooler						
Sea Glass						
Starfish						
Driftwood						
Silver Coin						
Sand Dollar						
Hermit Crab						

1. Eddie dug up his treasure with the tool he brought.
2. Kiera looked through the item she brought to see her sea glass.
3. The boy who carried the cooler put his driftwood inside.
4. Martha couldn't buy anything with her find. She put it in her bucket.
5. Jake was swimming with his toy when he found the hermit crab.
6. The girl who found the starfish put it on her towel.

AHOY!

Come sail away with us— or row, cruise, or float. We've gathered **21** kinds of watercraft. They can fit into the grid in just one way. Use the number of letters in each word to figure out where it belongs. Write in each name and cross it off the list as you go. *Bon voyage!*

4 Letters
RAFT
SCOW

5 Letters
BARGE
CANOE
FERRY
KAYAK
SCULL
YACHT

6 Letters
DINGHY
~~JET SKI~~

7 Letters
GONDOLA
PONTOON
ROWBOAT
TUGBOAT

8 Letters
LIFEBOAT
SAILBOAT

9 Letters
CATAMARAN
HOUSEBOAT
SPEED BOAT
STEAMBOAT

10 Letters
CRUISE SHIP

J E T S K I

Caving the Way

START

Can you help these hikers find the way out of the cave?
Find a clear path from START to FINISH. Watch out for bats!

FINISH

Illustrated by Steve Skelton

Mexico Search

¡*Hola!* We've collected 35 words that have to do with Mexico and its culture. There are cities, foods, historic sites, famous Mexicans, and more. To find them, look up, down, across, backwards, and diagonally. Have fun south of the border!

Word List

ACAPULCO

ADIOS

AMIGO

AZTEC

CANCUN

CASA

CHIPOTLE

CINCO DE MAYO

DAY OF THE DEAD

DIEGO RIVERA

ENCHILADA

FIESTA

GORDITA

HOLA

MAIZE

MARACA

MARIACHI

MASA

MAYA

MEXICO CITY

OAXACA

OCTAVIO PAZ

OLMEC

PANCHO VILLA

PESO

SALSA

SIESTA

SOMBRERO

SPANISH

TABASCO

TACO

TAMALE

TIJUANA

TORTILLA

YUCATAN

```
S I E S T A M E X I C O C I T Y
A T S E I F A L C H I P O T L E
L I H C A I R A M O O L V H W P
S D M A I Z E M M X C E M L O C
A F O Y T O V A A C A R A M S I
A Q A A I N I T D R T B V H E N
O B X M J O R E R B M O S M P C
C O A M U T O R T I L L A D A O
T L C J A T G B C B Q S H Q D D
A B A S N I E G G V A O O O A E
V Z Y K A T I D R O G I C A L M
I I T E Y B D K Y K F D L M I A
O Q K E B C A N C U N A U I H Y
P A V I C N A T A C U Y A P G C O
A S P A N I S H B E B Q A O N L F
Z A L L I V O H C N A P C R E F
S C D A Y O F T H E D E A D W H
```

Hidden Pictures® Arctic Beachgoers

banana

megaphone

crown

sailboat

teacup

ice-cream cone

party hat

glove

nail

fish

pencil

snake

heart

eagle's head

120

Illustrated by Tim Davis

Compass Comedy

Here's a puzzle that gets to the point! Start at the North (**N**) circle. Then move in the directions listed on the right. As you move to each new circle, write the letter you find there in the correct space. When you're done, read down the letters to find the answer to the riddle.

Why was the broom running late?

1. S 1 _____
2. SW 2 _____
3. SE 1 _____
4. E 3 _____
5. NW 2 _____
6. E 1 _____
7. N 1 _____
8. W 3 _____
9. S 4 _____
10. E 2 _____
11. NE 2 _____ .

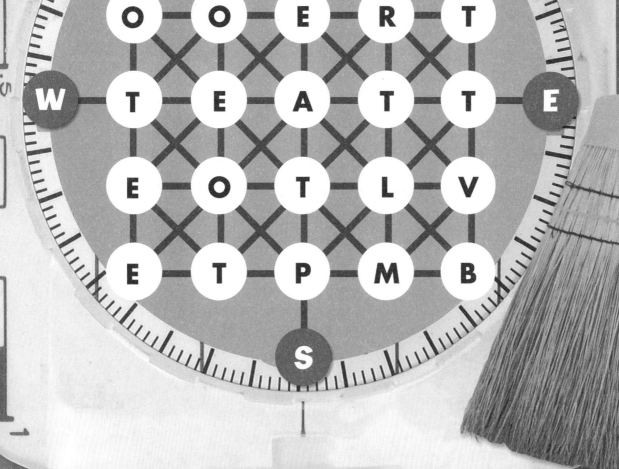

1:50,000 (km)   1:24,000 (miles)

Climb Every Mountain

Ten tall mountains are depicted on the next page. The list below has the name of each mountain along with its height in feet. Use the list to label each mountain peak with its proper name.

Kilimanjaro—(Africa) 19,340 feet

Pikes Peak (Rocky Mountains—North America) 14,110 feet

Mt. Rainier (Cascade Range—North America) 14,410 feet

Mt. Everest (Himalayas—Asia) 29,028 feet

Mt. Washington (White Mountains—North America) 6,288 feet

Mt. Mitchell (Appalachian Mountains—North America) 6,684 feet

Mt. Elbert (Rocky Mountains—North America) 14,433 feet

Mt. Marcy (Adirondack Mountains—North America) 5,344 feet

Aconcagua (Andes Mountains—South America) 22,834 feet

Mont Blanc (Alps—Europe) 15,771 feet

Illustrated by Scott Peck

China Q's

Dragon Dash

Li's team is trying to win the annual dragon boat race. Can you help them reach the finish line?

Start

Finish

Illustrated by Mike Moran

That's Lo-o-ong

The length of one famous Chinese structure is nearly twice the width of the Continental United States! To find out what the famous landmark is, write each set of colored letters on the lines below.

T W G C O R A H H L I E F N E A L T A

_____   _____   _____   _____   _____
RED   BLUE   ORANGE   PURPLE   GREEN

City Trivia

Can you match each Chinese city with its correct description?

1. Beijing
2. Shanghai
3. Hong Kong
4. Guangzhou

a. Chinese city with the largest population
b. Island territory off of mainland China
c. Host of the 2008 Summer Olympics
d. Fishing city near the Pacific Ocean

Light the Way

Colorful paper lanterns have been a tradition in China for thousands of years. Decorate your own lantern here!

Panda Twins

Some giant pandas still live in the wild in parts of China. Which two pictures are exactly alike?

Made in China

Five of these items were invented in China. Can you guess which ones?

Ice cream or Noodles?
Fireworks or Rocket ships?
Binoculars or Compass?
Paper or Plastic?
Silk or Wool?

Puzzles by Carly Schuna

125

Hidden Pictures®
Spike It!

Illustrated by Dave Klug

126

There is more than meets the eye in this beach volleyball game. Can you find the hidden objects?

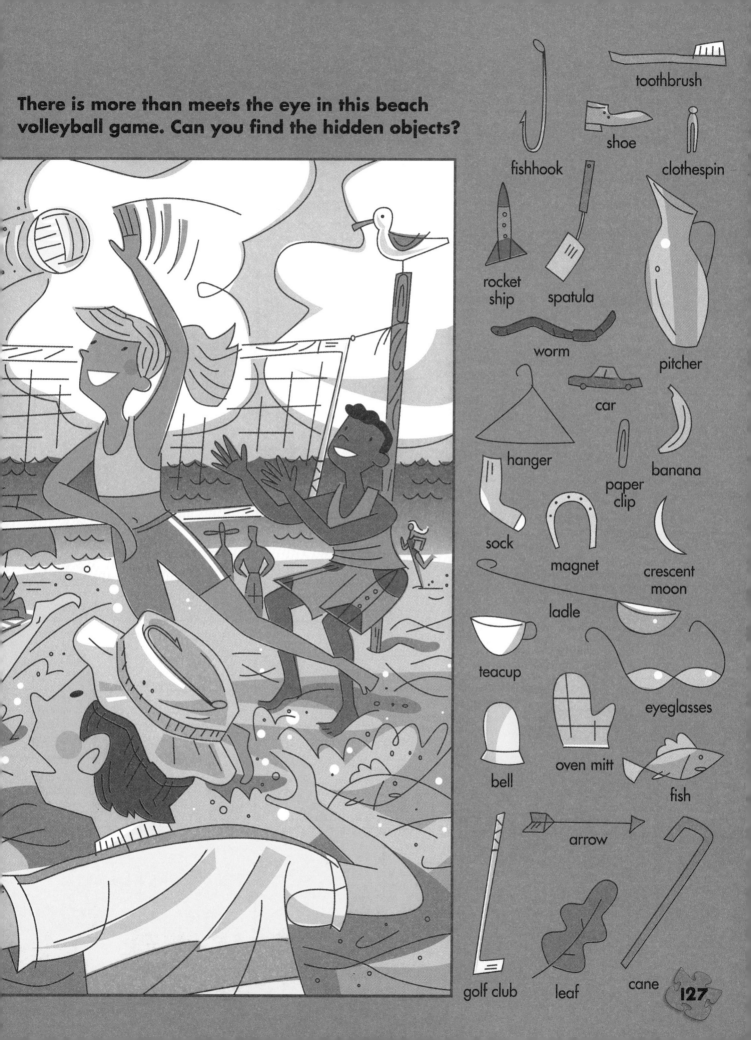

fishhook

toothbrush

shoe

clothespin

rocket ship

spatula

pitcher

worm

car

hanger

banana

paper clip

sock

magnet

crescent moon

ladle

teacup

eyeglasses

bell

oven mitt

fish

arrow

golf club

leaf

cane

Road Trip

Wanda and Rhonda are planning cross-country trips. They will both start in Los Angeles, California, and end in Washington, D.C. However, the roads they take and cities they

WANDA'S WAY

START

Los Angeles

San Diego

Phoenix

El Paso

Amarillo

Dallas

New Orleans

Birmingham

Atlanta

Knoxville

Washington, D.C.

RHONDA'S ROUTE

START

Los Angeles

Las Vegas

Salt Lake City

Denver

Oakley

Kansas City

Chicago

Indianapolis

Cincinnati

Charleston

Washington, D.C.

Salt Lake City

495

486

Denv

375

Las Vegas

Los
Angeles

124

San Diego

Phoenix

350

437

4

El P

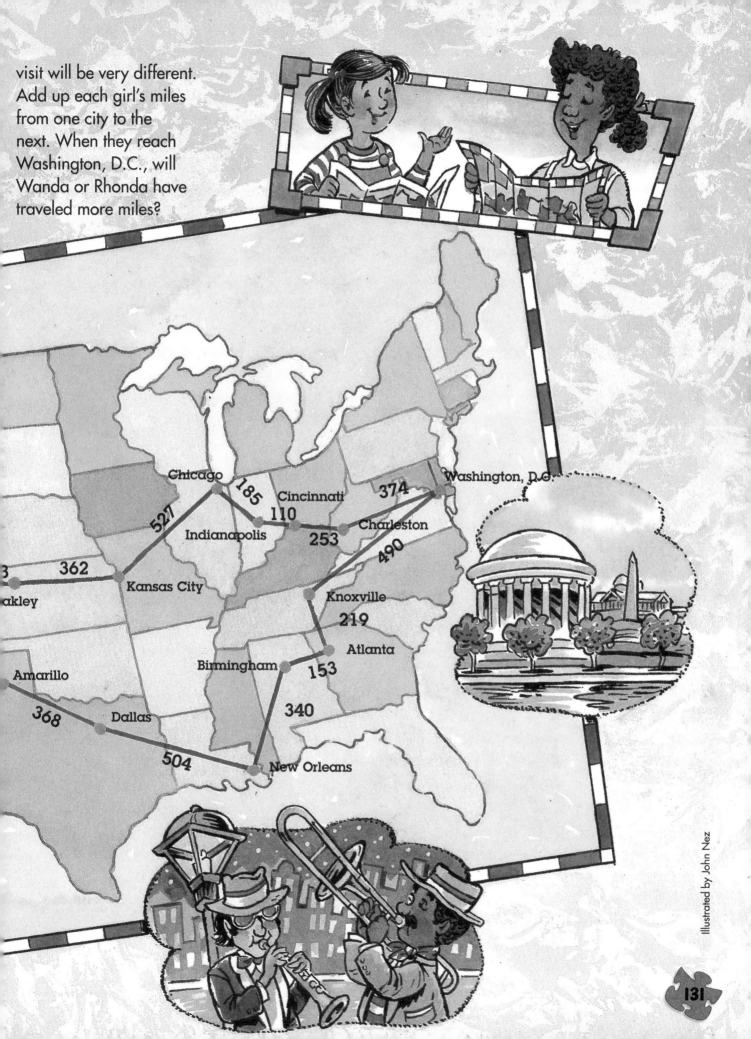

visit will be very different. Add up each girl's miles from one city to the next. When they reach Washington, D.C., will Wanda or Rhonda have traveled more miles?

Chicago
185
Cincinnati
374
Washington, D.C.
527
110
Indianapolis
Charleston
253
490
362
akley
Kansas City
Knoxville
219
Amarillo
Birmingham
Atlanta
153
368
Dallas
340
504
New Orleans

Illustrated by John Nez

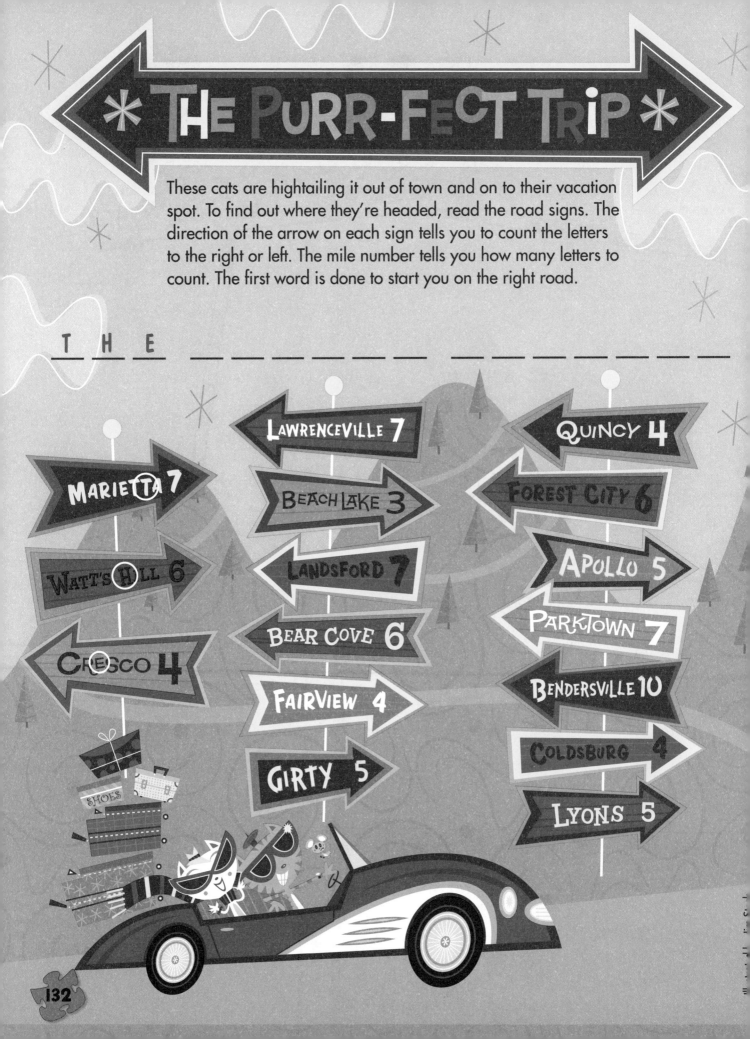

* THE PURR-FECT TRIP *

These cats are hightailing it out of town and on to their vacation spot. To find out where they're headed, read the road signs. The direction of the arrow on each sign tells you to count the letters to the right or left. The mile number tells you how many letters to count. The first word is done to start you on the right road.

T H E _ _ _ _ _ _ _ _ _ _ _ _

LAWRENCEVILLE 7

QUINCY 4

MARIETTA 7

BEACH LAKE 3

FOREST CITY 6

WATT'S HILL 6

LANDSFORD 7

APOLLO 5

BEAR COVE 6

PARKTOWN 7

CRESCO 4

FAIRVIEW 4

BENDERSVILLE 10

COLDSBURG 4

GIRTY 5

LYONS 5

SHOES

5 State Your Name

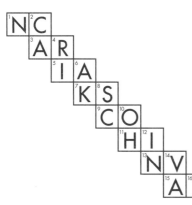

6–7 In Charge

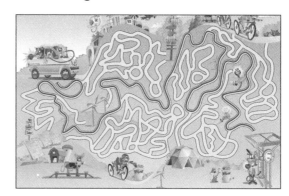

8–9 Surf's Up!

10–11 Capital Letters

12 Travel Trouble

13 Tic Tac Row

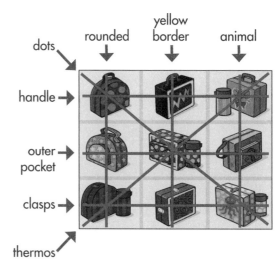

Answers

14–15 Lizard Lounging

18 Beach Read

16–17 California Q's

Freeway Free-for-All

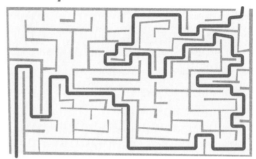

Missing Vowels

Hollywood
Yosemite National Park
Death Valley
Alcatraz
Big Sur

Cali Quiz

1. True   3. True
2. False   4. False

Bridge Twins

19 Family Vacations

Jennifer and William Green: NYC
Daniel and Emily King: Hawaii
Mia and Mike Peña: Alaska

20–21 Crisscross the U.S.A.

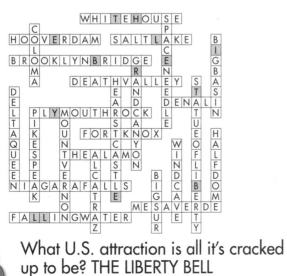

What U.S. attraction is all it's cracked up to be? THE LIBERTY BELL

24–25 Time Piece

1	2	3	4	5	6	7	8	9	10
11	12	13	14	15	16	17	18	19	20
21	22	23	24	25	26	27	28	29	30
31	32	33	34	35	36	37	38	39	40
41	42	43	44	45	46	47	48	49	50
51	52	53	54	55	56	57	58	59	60
61	62	63	64	65	66	67	68	69	70
71	72	73	74	75	76	77	78	79	80
81	82	83	84	85	86	87	88	89	90
91	92	93	94	95	96	97	98	99	100

The clock shows 3:00.

26–27 Hello, Lady Liberty

30–31 Lost Luggage

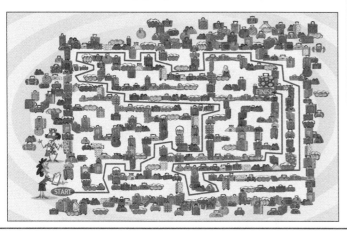

28–29 The Waiting Game

32–33 Park Here

34–35 Australia Q's

Return to Sender

Aussie Speak

Here is a sentence we made:
We had a bonzer barby this arvo near the billabong in the outback.

Dive In!

Here are the words we found. You may have found others.

age	brag	ferret	gear	raft	tiara
barge	ear	fire	grab	rib	tiger
bear	fair	free	grate	tear	tire
bite	fee	gate	greet	terrier	tree

'Doo This

Animals or Not?

Emu, Dingo, Koala, Wombat, Wallaby, Kookaburra

36–37 Sun and Shades

135

38–39 Digit Does It

Dear Uncle,

Don't be shocked, but we hid all the shells. You'll have to exercise your "shellf"-control to find all 25. Sorry to be so "shell"-fish.

Love, Denise and Deneffew Digit

42 Country Sudoku

F	R	A	N	C	E
E	N	C	A	F	R
R	A	E	C	N	F
N	C	F	R	E	A
C	F	R	E	A	N
A	E	N	F	R	C

T	U	R	K	E	Y
E	Y	K	U	R	T
U	E	Y	T	K	R
K	R	T	E	Y	U
Y	K	U	R	T	E
R	T	E	Y	U	K

B	R	A	Z	I	L
L	Z	I	R	A	B
Z	A	B	I	L	R
I	L	R	B	Z	A
A	B	Z	L	R	I
R	I	L	A	B	Z

40–41 Seeing i to i

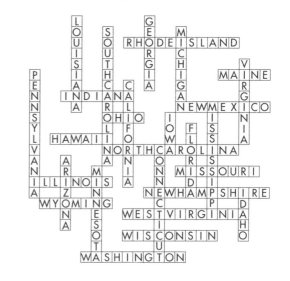

43 A Tall Taxi

44–45 To New Depths

Monday: 150 feet
Tuesday: 275 feet
Wednesday: 325 feet
Thursday: 175 feet
Friday: 412.5 feet
Total for the week: 1,337.5 feet

46–47 Beware Bears

48–49 Pier Cheer

50–51 Rapid Repeat

54–55 Tugboat Travels

Dock 1: 4 people on board
Island 2: $(4 - 1) + 2 = 5$
Island 3: $5 - 3 = 2$
Island 4: $(2 + 3) - 1 + (2 + 1) = 7$
Island 5: $7 + 2 = 9$
Island 6: $9 - 1 = 8$
Island 7: $8 - 2 = 6$
Island 8: $6 - 3 = 3$
Island 9: $3 - 2 = 1$

What kind of boat will the captain use to move the elephants?

AN EXTRA-LARGE BARGE

56–57 Castle Search

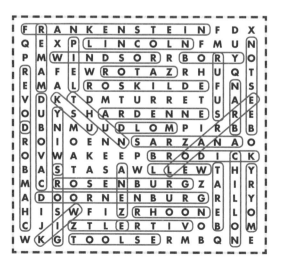

52–53 City Q's

Guess What?

It's the Space Needle in Seattle, Washington.

Europe or Asia

EUROPE:	ASIA:
Madrid	Mumbai
Venice	Bangkok
London	Seoul
Paris	Tokyo
Amsterdam	Hong Kong

Jumbled Cities

SEATTLE, Washington
DALLAS, Texas
BALTIMORE, Maryland
ANCHORAGE, Alaska
MINNEAPOLIS, Minnesota

Twin Taxis

Taxi cabs A and D are exactly alike.

Also Known As...

CHICAGO • THE WINDY CITY

DETROIT • MOTOWN

NASHVILLE • MUSIC CITY

NEW ORLEANS • THE BIG EASY

NEW YORK CITY • THE BIG APPLE

PHILADELPHIA • THE CITY OF BROTHERLY LOVE

Rush Hour

60–61 A Whale of a Time

137

Answers

62-63 Mayan Maze

64-65 On Sail

66 Car Campers

67 Tic Tac Row

flag →   house ↓   ladder and two windows ↓   stripe ↓

black roof →

seagulls →

light →

boat ↗

68-69 Wild Times

70-71 Hawaii Q's

Hot Hike

Twin Leis

Leis A and D are exactly alike.

Hawaii or Not?

Hilo, Maui, Kauai, Oahu, Waipahu, Honolulu, Kona

Aloha!

Here is a sentence we made up: Today at the kai, I saw a nui honu swimming wikiwiki in the wai.

Missing Vowels

BANANA
PINEAPPLE
COCONUT
MANGO
PASSION FRUIT

72–73 Lodging Logic

548: Rhodes   789: Quinns

865: Karrs   532: Dukes

533: O'Nighters   874: Princes

703: Kings   800: Travellis

74 World Pieces

1. Canada   7. Thailand
2. China   8. Ethiopia
3. Sweden   9. Costa Rica
4. Turkey   10. United States
5. Ireland   11. South Africa
6. Germany   12. Argentina

75 Aloha!

K	O	N	N	I	C	H	I	W	A		
	A							I	T	A	
	M			G				T			
C	I	A	O	O				A			
	S			D		J	A	M	B	O	
	T			D					O	N	
G	U	T	E	N	T	A	G			N	J
	D		I		A		G			O	
	A		H			S	H	A	L	O	M
Y	I	A	S	A	S		O			U	
				O			L			R	
			S	A	L	A	A	M			

76–77 Rolling on the River

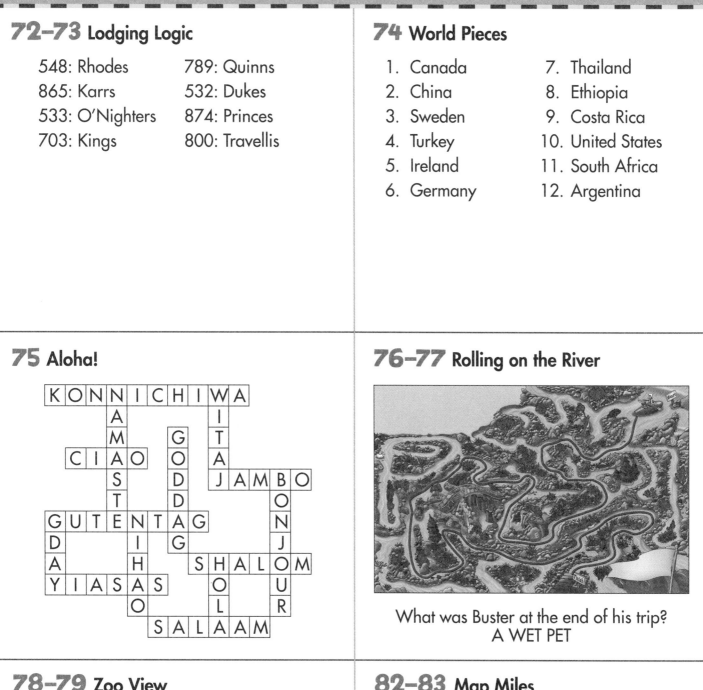

What was Buster at the end of his trip?
A WET PET

78–79 Zoo View

82–83 Map Miles

Trip 1—45 miles
(Eagle Tower to Blufftown to Cedar Springs
to Lakeside to Rapid River to Sandtown)

Trip 2—19 miles
(Wood to Pine City to Lakeside)

Trip 3—31 miles
(Blue City to Big Bay to Rapid River
to Lakeside to Cedar Springs)

Trip 4—27 miles
(Big Bay to Pine City to Rockville to Blufftown)

Trip 5—20 miles
(Rapid River to Lakeside to Rockville)

139

84–85 Italy Search

86 Family Ties

Alyssa: New York, 12

Brad: Iowa, 10

Catie: New Mexico, 9

Daniel: Maine, 6

Eve: California, 8

87 Aerial View

88–89 Vacation Q's

Pool Plunge

Where Am I?	Jumbled Packing
Liberty Bell	book
Space Needle	shorts
Grand Canyon	camera
Niagara Falls	swimsuit
Plymouth Rock	sunglasses

Hit the Road

Lincoln Memorial	Washington, D.C.
Old Faithful	Wyoming
Statue of Liberty	New York
Mount Rushmore	South Dakota
Gateway Arch	Missouri
The Alamo	Texas

Trip Trios

90–91 Go...Go...Gorilla!

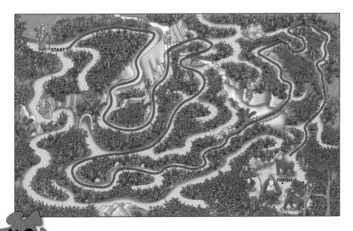

92–93 Digit Does It

Dear Inspector Digit,

Peter Pickpocket picked a pack of pockets. If Peter picked a pair of pockets per person and each pocket produced a pair of pennies, how many pennies did Peter pick?

Twelve people times two pockets each is 24 pockets. Multiply that by two pennies per pocket for a total of 48 pennies.

94–95 Coral Explorers

96–97 Aussie Animals

98–99 Island Rides

1 = 2 ÷ 2

2 = 0 + 2

3 = 1 + 2

4 = 2 x 2

5 = 10 ÷ 2

6 = 2 x 3

7 = 5 + 2

8 = (2 x 2) x 2

9 = 11 – 2

10 = (2 x 2) x 2 + 2

11 = 22 ÷ 2

12 = (2 x 2) x (2 + 1)

100–101 Up, Up, and Away!

102 Tic Tac Row

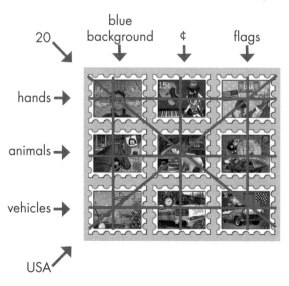

103 Are We There Yet?

141

Answers

106–107 Egypt Q's

On the Nile

Boy King
Here are the words we found.
You may have found others.

ant	hut	tank
aunt	man	than
ham	mat	that
hat	mutt	thank
hum	nut	tutu
human	tan	

Egypt or Not?
Luxor
Giza
Cairo
Ismailia
Alexandria
Suez
Tanta

Jumbled Egypt
Nile
mummy
Sahara
Sphinx
pyramid

Twin Sphinxes

108–109 Island Hopping

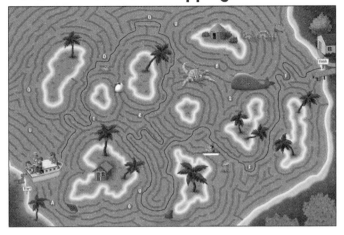

Why don't dogs like being on boats?
Because the waters are TOO RUFF!

110–111 Mount Rushmore

112–113 On the Road Again

From home to Shelbyville	57 miles
Shelbyville to Capital City	143 miles
Capital City to Springfield	105 miles
Springfield to Edwardsville	84 miles
Edwardsville to Morgantown	61 miles
Morgantown to home	210 miles
TOTAL MILES	660 miles

**At 30 miles per gallon,
Rhoda will use 22 gallons.**

114 Treasure Beach

Jake: fins, hermit crab
Eddie: shovel, silver coin
Braden: cooler, driftwood
Haley: towel, starfish
Martha: bucket, sand dollar
Kiera: goggles, sea glass

115 Ahoy!

116–117 Caving the Way

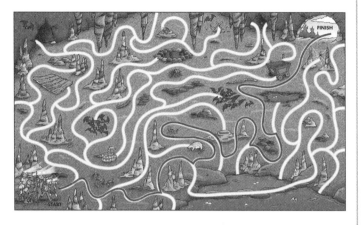

120 Arctic Beachgoers

122–123 Climb Every Mountain

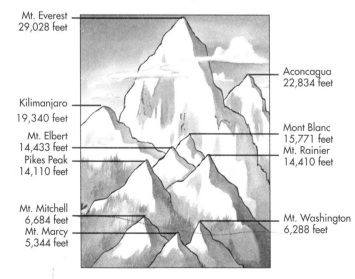

Mt. Everest 29,028 feet
Aconcagua 22,834 feet
Kilimanjaro 19,340 feet
Mont Blanc 15,771 feet
Mt. Elbert 14,433 feet
Mt. Rainier 14,410 feet
Pikes Peak 14,110 feet
Mt. Mitchell 6,684 feet
Mt. Washington 6,288 feet
Mt. Marcy 5,344 feet

118–119 Mexico Search

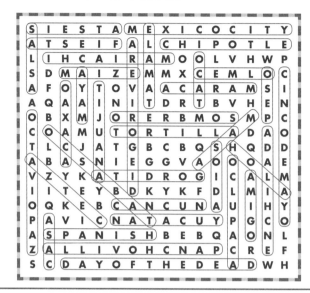

121 Compass Comedy

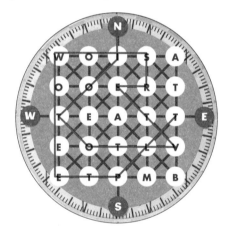

Why was the broom running late?
IT OVERSWEPT.

124–125 China Q's

Dragon Dash

That's Lo-o-ong
THE GREAT WALL OF CHINA

City Trivia

1. c
2. a
3. b
4. d

Panda Twins

Made in China

Noodles
Fireworks
Compass
Paper
Silk

143

126–127 Spike It!

128–129 City Traffic

130–131 Road Trip

WANDA'S WAY		RHONDA'S ROUTE	
START		START	
Los Angeles		Los Angeles	
San Diego	124	Las Vegas	375
Phoenix	350	Salt Lake City	486
El Paso	437	Denver	495
Amarillo	421	Oakley	253
Dallas	368	Kansas City	362
New Orleans	504	Chicago	527
Birmingham	340	Indianapolis	185
Atlanta	153	Cincinnati	110
Knoxville	219	Charleston	253
Washington, D.C.	490	Washington, D.C.	374
	3,406		3,420

Wanda went 3,406 miles and
Rhonda went 3,420 miles, so
Rhonda's trip was longer by 14 miles.

132 The Purr-fect Trip

The cats went to THE CANARY ISLANDS.